FROM NOTHING

Also by Daniel Tobin

Poetry

The Net
Belated Heavens
Second Things
The Narrows
Double Life
Where the World Is Made

Criticism

Awake in America
Passage to the Center: Imagination and the Sacred in the Poetry of
Seamus Heaney

Editor

The Book of Irish American Poetry from the Eighteenth Century
to the Present
Light in Hand: Selected Early Poems of Lola Ridge
Poet's Work, Poet's Play: Essays on the Practice and the Art
(with Pimone Triplett)

FROM NOTHING

Daniel Tobin

Four Way Books
Tribeca

Please direct all inquiries to:
Editorial Office
Four Way Books
POB 535, Village Station
New York, NY 10014
www.fourwaybooks.com

Library of Congress Cataloging-in-Publication Data

Tobin, Daniel.
From nothing : a poem / by Daniel Tobin.
pages ; cm
ISBN 978-1-935536-69-7 (softcover : acid-free paper)
I. Title.
PS3570.O289F76 2016
811'.54--dc23

2015028573

This book is manufactured in the United States of America and printed on acid-free paper.

Four Way Books is a not-for-profit literary press. We are grateful for the assistance
we receive from individual donors, public arts agencies, and private foundations.

This publication is made possible with public funds from the New York State Council on the Arts,
a state agency.

[clmp]

We are a proud member of the Community of Literary Magazines and Presses.

Distributed by University Press of New England
One Court Street, Lebanon, NH 03766

Contents

(Stream)   "Jubilant billowing from the choir loft, throngs in song"

(Nexus)   "To you even so comes the open door, to commune"

(Contratemps)   "All one, one would believe, and *Behind Every Door*"

(Agnus)   "Mary had little lambda. His fleece was Jesus—Ha!"

(Anthropic)   "This process of coming to life: autocatalysis of wave"

(Cinema)   "In the film that doesn't begin and never ends, a man"

(Spiritus)   "Stylus, number wheel, gear tooth, cog, a falling weight"

(Corpus)   "For all of it, how presumptuous, we thinking reeds "

(Canto)   "*Is it motion itself that makes the day? Or is it the time*"

(Matins)   "*Mon ami, mon frère*, in the trenches nearly *mon semblable*"

(Cove)   "Sometimes it's no different than the sound of the surf"

". . .and the universe nothing more than dream. . ."

Georges Lemaître (1894-1966)

Georges Lemaître was a Belgian mathematician, theoretical physicist,
and Jesuit priest whose insights during the 1930s and 1940s provided
solutions to physical problems stemming from Einstein's general theory
of relativity and quantum mechanics that Einstein himself did not foresee.
Though a lesser-known figure in cosmology, he was the first to develop
a theory of an expanding universe through the explosion of a "primeval
atom," what has become known popularly as "the big bang." He was
the first to recognize the validity of the cosmological constant (lambda)
as a gravitationally repulsive force that explains the current acceleration
of cosmic expansion, and the first to offer mathematical solutions that
anticipated the discovery of black holes. He envisioned, in short, the most
scientifically robust theory of the universe before the discovery of cosmic
microwave background radiation, the CMB, which he predicted, as well as
the theory of inflation that has emerged from "big bang" theory.
While there is sublimity in Lemaître's scientific and mathematical genius,
his life also intersects intimately and crucially with the 20th century's
most profound historical and human catastrophes. A devotee of the 14th
century Flemish mystic, Jan van Ruysbroeck, Lemaître was likewise a
pioneer of computer programming and modeling. Georges Lemaître died
on the cusp of the summer solstice, a week after being told of Penzias and
Wilson's discovery of the CMB, the fossil light that is quietly and indelibly
present in all quarters of the sky.

And to one God says: Come
to me by numbers and
figures: see my beauty
in the angles between
stars, in the equations
of my kingdom. . .

      And to another:
I am the bush burning
at the center of
your existence. . .

R.S. Thomas, "Meditations"

From Nothing

A World-Line in Thirty-Three Takes

. . . this sudden stirring, like birds before
an earthquake, then the explosion—

a fluency of wine in water, white streak
across a white vault of sky where the tunnel

opens to Bright Abounding, its utter light,
fleet release, ecstatic, unutterable, before. . .

The Most Ancient Light in the Most Ancient Sky

We may speak of this event as a beginning; I do not say a creation. . . . Any preexistence of the universe has a metaphysical character. Physically, everything happens as if the theoretical zero was really a beginning. The question if it was really a beginning or rather a creation, something started from nothing, is a philosophical question which cannot be settled by physical or astronomical considerations.

—Georges Lemaître

(Fountain)

To figure from nothing, holiness in perihelion:
though one must not proclaim it, but let the matter
spin along its poles into the bright entanglements,

like two particles of light flung to opposite zones,
and still the one moves with and how the other moves—
love's choreography in the elegance of the dance.

Though maybe it's more like matter and antimatter,
the one canceling the other in a blinding negation,
number and *noumen* locked in their separate estates.

You would not collapse them to a point's white heat,
but kept them before you, your physics and your faith,
the divergent roads with their singular horizon

where the radius of space converges into zero,
where what was, is, will be waxes without boundary
into seed and sand grain, a Cepheid luster of eyes—

news of the minor signature keyed from everywhere,
the primal radiation, omnipresent, the prodigal
wave arriving from its Now that has no yesterday,

the proof of your calculus, the tour of the expanse:
"The evolution of the universe might be compared
to a display of fireworks that has just ended,

some few red wisps, ashes and smoke. So we stand
on a well-cooled cinder to see the fading of suns,
to glimpse a vanished brilliance, the origin of worlds."

(Origin)

A little sand, a little soda, a little lime once used
to embalm the dead, and out of black hole and kiln
the molten bubble gathers like honey on a dipper

for the blower to stretch breath into glass, the pipe
a silent horn shaping the form with its emptiness
to be marvered and mandrelled, jacked and lathed.

In your father's factory the vessels anneal, neat rows
of flagons, jars, mould blown, ribbed and decorated,
every glinted edge and pattern the fire will destroy

so the life foreseen becomes a retrospect foreknown:
the char-black rolling country of the Pays Noir
from which your people came—the smelting works

and coal pits, gas, slag-heap, pick-axe and sump.
He rose from all that, and rose again to make good
for the losses, for his laborers, as though justice

were the standard candle he followed in the dark,
or the hidden vein in a seam of earth that opens
on a vault where monstrance lifts from the monstrous.

In the photographer's studio your mother nestles you
on folded cloth, an heir of miners and weavers,
the scene a tapestry of hills and fields and settling sky.

You could be a girl in your frilled gown, or Rilke,
your eyes as bright and lenient, your right hand
gesturing outward, the left already figuring sums.

(Fiat)

In the Cathedral Saint-Michel, the chancel window
pours down its lucid spectrum across the altar.
The priest in green chasuble for Ordinary Time

bows before the tabernacle, paten, chalice, *Agnus Dei*.
Uniformly you sit among the pews and schoolboys.
Latin and incense commingle beneath the nave.

The altar servers in their chiaroscuro—white surplice,
black soutane—move in consort to cross and ciborium.
Is it now that you sense the certainty of your calling?

Or had it haunted you nights with your schoolbooks
even back in Charleroi, in the halls of Sacré Coeur:
calculation and consecration, geometry and God?

"There is nothing I think in all of physical reality
more abstruse than the doctrine of the Trinity,"
you would write years later, your primeval quantum

inflating to millennia, into weeks and days:
if only every life, like quires in a Book of Hours,
could unfold from vellum, unique and indelible.

In the glittering fan the priest lifts host and chalice,
bread and wine to body and blood, as though a switch
flickered at the bottom of things, its sizzling foam,

with a word accidence into essence alchemized.
While outside immaculate gardens begin to bloom
in riots of light, pallets of flesh, stained glass blazoning.

(De Rerum)
Georges Lemaître

"A red flare broadcasts its annunciation over the Salient,
Ypres in the half-light of morning, an unnatural silence
broken by the screech of shrapnel shell and howitzer,

machine guns spattering the parapets of No Man's Land.
Horrible enough the slaughter, hand to hand, house to house,
in Lombartzyde—bayonet, rifle shot, the blood in my nails.

We've opened the sea sluices to hold back their onslaught,
Louvain burned, this one strip left of free Belgium.
Now these crater fields, the men mown down in swathes.

Why is it, O my Precious Christ, we do this to each other,
crouching in transverse, trench, the barbed, deadlocked lines,
who might have joined like harvesters among hedge and fold?

A hiss, and from enemy dug-outs the strange cloud curls
in waves, grayish, yellow to green, darkest at the bottom.
And I know we are in a biblical plague, the men fumbling

for bits of flannel, cotton pads, the gassed in spasm, clawing
at their throats, their eyes, vomiting, crawling off to die—
the way the forsaken do in Bruegel's *The Triumph of Death,*

its black plumes of smoke and burning cities, its scythes
and armies, skeletal, their coffin lid shields, the slit throats,
wagonloads of skulls, that dog nibbling a dead child's face.

On the ravaged plain, a cauldron of torture and carnage
like ours with its mangles, stumps, stench, and splintered trees,
the Cross still rises skyward, Death hammering the plinth."

(Parallax)

To have lived inside wrath: *Croix de Guerre:* the continent
a slaughterhouse. To have borne it, strafes, gas, liquid fire,
to have come through—by what turn of Catherine wheel,

by what hand? While other minds were ground to chaff.
You calculating the cosines of targets, trajectories,
in the rare calm reading Poincaré in trench and redoubt,

time synchronized with space in telegraph and meridian,
cables under crisscrossed oceans, the swung pendulums
mastering prime, Schwartzchild dead at the East Front,

Moseley in Gallipoli, and De Sitter with his universe
emptied mathematically of matter in order to conjure
mass and energy in motion—our inhabited world.

Gone the ether with its airy thinness cicatrizing light,
planets, those "wild sheep," in daisy chains of epicycles
dervishing a centered earth. Newton's apple plunges

down the parallax of a rabbit hole, its wake a bend
of starlight tacking the halo of an eclipsed sun
and clocks ticking tick to the measure of every eye:

the genius's equation like a single stone launched
to shatter the foundations. So you teach yourself tensor,
mastering scales, and limp through Aquinas' *Summa.*

So in three years: your perpetual vows, your first Mass.
Introibo ad altare Dei. Ad Gloriam. You lift the cup—
in its shivering well the horizon of the Hidden.

(Trajectory)

I have known the dreadful dissolution, seen all
perish again and again, every atom dissolved
into the fathomless, the wild infinity, an ocean

emptied of everything. Utter darkness. Who can count
the creations that have passed away, the creations
risen afresh in the eye-blink eons of the Puranas?

And in this, our newest fraught iteration,
on Sobral and Principe, crews ready plates to catch
the moon's black coin dissolve the sun. Island hush.

Occultation. Radiant corona. Behind the blaze
arc-seconds of stars while Eddington deduces proof,
the known strata of the physical phase-shifted

to uncertainty in the slimmest bending of light.
He would play the universe—a symphony scaled
in constants, seven harmonic notes, link electron

to galaxy in the finest structures, unfathomable
as Bottom's bottomless dream, and mentored you,
his protégé, the "plump priest" with your collar

circumspect, with your speculations plumb: *I found*
M. Lemaître a very brilliant student, clear-sighted,
wonderfully quick. And you at the border of naught:

"We can think of a convex polyhedron, enclosing
all stars, all particles of which matter is formed,
the universe a bubble dipped in a sea of nothingness."

(Scope)

So let there be Shakespeare: *I have had a most rare*
vision—I have had a dream—past the wit of man
to say what dream this was: In St. Edmund's you parse

the puzzle of simultaneity where two events
accelerating uniformly in curved space veer
as Einstein believed into their relative intervals,

and one's face traveling at light speed vanishes
from the mirror before one, for nothing arrives
let alone is reflected till it gets where it's going:

and no master clock evident, no synchronous
tick, though trains leave their stations, elevators
plunge in their arrow vacuum good as standing still,

while you accelerate on your own trajectory:
Cambridge to Harvard, the Observatory's dome,
its brass eye ranging at a crest of winding stairs,

its cannonballs for bearings, Shapley charging you
to track the variables, spectra, the radial velocities:
MIT, Dominion, Lowell, Mount Wilson, each scope

opening the gathering vistas of nuance and error—
as though the painted desert you witness with Slipher,
its bends and colors, its outsized beauty and scale,

were the bright figure of your incipient sublime,
by datum to datum mastering the farthest fields,
one grain accomplishing vastness in a torrid noon.

(Vector)

In a life below decks in a great ship, windowless,
butterflies in lamplight are moving as they move.
Fish swim indifferently inside their bowl, two men

toss a ball, each to each, as the ship speeds, head-
long ahead, and nothing's driven back to the stern
since to go with this motion is to be moored in port.

From the tallest mountain at the mind's white pole
a cannon fires its charges into space, progressive
speed, till one ball, by falling, flies, by flying, falls.

Now the surfer catches a wave of frozen light
and rides it motionless to an impossible shore
where he reckons sand the particles of his path:

and twins, one traveled from earthbound earth,
the other staying home, meet again after years,
each to the other younger from when he left.

The cat in its dire box keeps equally live and dead,
the poison released, should hammer shatter flask
when the atom decays, which it may not, or it may.

You, who chose two ways equally at once, circuit
the conferences, meetings fueled by enigma,
mixing with the eminent and their sidereal regard,

your morning Masses before library and lab.
All outcomes must be possible in the system—Schrödinger.
In your life's chosen box, this con-celebration.

(Proscenium)

"We can compare space-time to an open, conic cup. . ."
at bottom: the first instant, the now with no before.
Or say galaxies are dots on a balloon's inflating skin,

the telescope a time machine, the past an aperture,
our looking out, away, a way of looking back.
It's not what he had hoped to hear, the maestro

of the Patent Office, the machine maker's son
who had undone every absolute and wanted still
a universe like a glass sphere balancing on a pin..

And so, at Solvay, you approach him in the park.
You, with your "dog-collar," face the genius' rebuff:
Your calculations are correct, your physics abominable.

But how then explain the Dog Star's parallax,
geometries of curved space, its broken symmetry,
the brightly fleeting spectra of Kant's island worlds?

At the Metropole, dignitaries back from talks
haunt smoking room and club. Emergent autumn
with its hints of rust, brightness hurtling to the brink.

You walk the winding pathways of the Leopold
noting gardens dying back, the rare, un-leafing trees,
mallards on Maalbeek pond mirrored with sky,

that rose-ringed parakeet on its branch, errant
from the habitat of its origin and still at home:
"There are two paths to truth; I have chosen both."

(Observance)
Edwin Hubble

"Tall, strong, beautiful, with the shoulders of Hermes
of Praxiteles, that is how my wife first fashioned me,
I who proved our Milky Way but another galaxy

among the *Nebelflecken* fleeing breakneck with the rest
by the law, the constant, the time that bear my name:
Hubble, stamped with Newton, Copernicus, Galileo.

Not bad for an Ozark farm boy hodded off to Oxford
on a Rhodes, who tailored himself to tweeds and speaks
the King's English, as though he'd suckled on shires.

Astronomy, I attest, is a history of receding horizons,
though mine tend to open to dinners with Stravinsky,
the Fairbanks, and *coup de maître*, my surprise star-turn

at the Oscars: spotlights, applause, the whole heavens
blue-shifted to me. Still—nothing headier than nights
on Mt. Wilson, eye at the lens, my briar pipe glowing,

Humason at the spectrascope tracing the light shifts
who was my mule driver. His habits—straight poker,
panther juice—try the soul, but he's brilliant at the shot.

Odd, too, the little priest who came to visit years ago,
that he should account for nebulas' radial velocities
two years before me, though I only trust the data—

how he looked calmly pleased at Einstein's recantation:
The most beautiful solution to creation I have ever heard.
So clocks reel back with space—camera, action, light."

(Shore)

Along the dune-sidled folds of the *plage*, the waves
roil imperturbably their endless perturbations:
Der Haan, West Flanders. Where in legend a rooster

crowed to save the drowning in a wreck off shore.
Where in *la belle époque* kings came to gab and golf.
Where, now, you visit the genius, exiled with his family,

for whom Germany has become death, the warrant
signed by the new Führer—calls to kill the pacifist
whose cosmos is brainchild of "The Eternal Jew."

The military system is the worst outcrop of herd nature,
your new friend will write, and *I hold pure thought
a great reality as the ancients dreamed*—on this shore

contemplating the field, or practicing the violin.
Now, as at the Athenaeum, you roll a cigarette,
peeling apart your own to replenish his store

while bodyguards walk behind. *It was the experience
of mystery—even mixed with fear—that engendered
religion, the existence of something we cannot penetrate.*

But in that thought: nature's reason alone, the eternity
of this world, alone, its marvelous structure, no God,
and life beyond death the absurd desire of feeble souls.

And you? "In the face of suffering, we must drop books
and pray." Nothing crows from the dunes. The sea,
the seething littoral, churns for its night of broken glass.

14

The Death of One God is the Death of All

I believe in Spinoza's God who reveals himself in the harmony of all that exists, but not in a God who concerns himself with the fate and actions of human beings.

—Albert Einstein

(Melisma)

One note, another, in the parlor's angled light:
your fingers flaring across keys, the waiting clavier,
its felt hammers striking strings, resonant frequency

borne from score to bridge to sounding board,
coupling every gradient of energy into air.
So your moments fill with the shapeliness of song

here in the safe flat beside the Town Hall, its façade
a medieval choreography of burghers, saints,
secular cathedral, while the Reich's page turners

goose-step through your streets. You saw, advancing,
this second coming, the library at Louvain again
a torched sanctum, melted webs of steel, charred cocoon.

You'd have made your way to the coast, Pas-de-Calais,
and over the channel, father, mother in tow,
would have beaten to the pass the panzers at Dunkirk

that turned you back and locked you in retreat.
In Princeton Einstein has written his letter, his fear
of atoms concerted to bombs by German hands,

the President in seclusion committing the secret funds.
Now this bright November sun of Berchtesgaden,
the neutral king portioning his pact with Hitler.

Is there a providence at the heart of quantum chance,
the risk of the Pianist whose score evolves the keys?
Point and purpose hazarded on scales across scales.

(Calculus)

Now in earshot of you—the scale that shatters scales:
50 freight cars x 50 per car x 1.5 trains per day
x 1066 days = 4,000,000 Jews "resettled to the East"

exclusive of the death squads, and each one eclipsed
behind the death gate's limit, its prevailing West,
and Himmler petitioning the Minister of Transport

"I must have more trains": among them cattle cars
out of Brussels, out of Antwerp via Breendonck
and Malines—your seminary within hailing distance

of the moated barracks where Öbersturnführer Asche
assembles them for Auschwitz, Berkenau, Bergen-Belsen:
Asche to ash along the side line track through Louvain.

That fall afternoon, your father collapses on a tram
and the one who sits beside him wears a yellow star.
We have the duty of conscience to strive for resistance

declares His Holiness Van Roey. And you, good son
charged to attend your mother, leaven act with prayer
like an untestable theorem, listening into the vacuum.

But to see the singularity in a sphere composed of dust,
to see beyond the given limit to the horizon where light
plunges permanently into the void: your "dust solution"

by which space and time contract to nil—how to reconcile
the math when the metaphor waxes real, gravity, graves,
cinder clouds, a calculus of stars red shifting on the rails?

(Chamber)

Sunflower plumage, a pulsing body alive with song:
the Pope's canary, perched ex cathedra on his shoulder,
sings nothing of what is past, or passing, or to come.

Gretchen, his favorite, freed from her cage, keeps vigil
there, while Pius, rail-thin, pallid as a plaster saint,
eats alone according to his habit, the staunch observance

of his solitude, that lifted gaze for which he is revered.
Scholar, classicist, holy man, bureaucrat, former nuncio
to the Reich, invoker of conclaves and concordats:

should he speak the word that utters condemnation
to the bestial, the antichrist? And him the Vicar of Christ
caught in the inertia of his prudence, his well-meant

action at a distance that would preserve his own tribe,
or risk the fury, martyrdom, His Church a shambles?
The laws which bind civilized people together

have been violated, he broadcasts on Christmas,
his rhetoric a dark wood veiling Buchenwald,
the telegrams to Hitler, his silence at the roundups

near Vatican walls: culpability caught by hindsight,
the encyclical denouncing hate shelved for diplomacy.
In the photograph you look up at him, your pontiff,

as he welcomes you, obedient, open, to his throne.
And had *he* donned the yellow star? History's "What if."
O golden haired Margaret, O ashen haired Shulamith.

(Aperture)

And so, let the mind commit a thought experiment,
split the physicist from priest like a single photon
shot through a screen, charting the divergent paths:

—"Consider a civilization where music is unknown,
only acoustics and frequencies, the notes like an air
un-breathable for the animal in its element.

Is this not where our method leads us, into matter
as matter, force as force, the amplitudes a blank smoke
unnecessary—number as number and nothing more?"

—"Infinity is such an artistic creation, all symmetry
and elegance, but your method smacks of metaphysics,
lifeless life, and the Bible is not a textbook of science.

If relativity theory had been necessary to salvation
it would have been revealed to St. Paul or Moses.
Still, the deeper we penetrate the universal mystery

the more we will find one law and one goodness."
—"Newton's *Principia*, Abbe Mendel and his peas,
from quantum to quanta—all purposeless process."

—"Time's arrow at t=0 has a barb at each end
that makes the infinite universe a buried corpse.
Our world is now a world where something happens,

with the world's matter present from the beginning,
with the world's story to be written step by step."
—"In venom, crematoria, the animal's voided blood."

(Tenebrae)

This shadowgraph performance of familiar life, shadow
of an elbow on a shadow table, the shadow ink flowing
over shadow paper, the body no more than a spectral

orchestration, specks whirling with specks in a greater
emptiness, within, without, the fragile, mutable matter
of ourselves, flotsam from the quantum sea, emergent,

or devolved from some more perfect symmetry, broken
into world-lines and geodesics, cathedral-webs of space,
and time, statistical magician, pulls a rabbit from its hat: us.

God does not play dice with the universe, but where is
Der Alte when you need Him? Newton's Divine Observer
letting each passing, solitary, sum-over-history break

on Him, with our local sufferings, astride the non-local:
the solving, unsatisfying, tunneling path of letting it happen?
So, on the mesa, the Sangre de Cristo a roiling geometry

of light and shade, the Lord Rapid Rupture assembles
the luminaries, subcritical mass to critical mass,
to ensure the Bomb's tamper attains maximal efficiency.

And you, forgotten in your shadow-life in the outskirts
of Hell, consider the passage you struck years before:
"I think that everyone who believes in a supreme being

supporting every life, every action, believes that God
is essentially hidden, and may be glad also to see
how present physics provides a veil hiding the creation."

(Sanctum)

Darkness on the face of the deep, darkness hidden
by darkness, no time before time, before existence
and non-existence, but to climb as the mystic said

to the high mountains, where there is no shadow,
only sun. So in mind you reverse the symmetry
to walk beside him in Grönendael, green valley,

with his tablet and stylus to the Soignes' axel tree
where clarity shines with the exactness of equations,
his soul become a live coal in the fire of infinite love

by which he sees through the multiplicity of things:
To know it we must be in it, beyond the mind, above
our created being, in that Eternal Point where all

our lines begin and end, where they lose their name,
become that very One the Point is, and yet remain
themselves nought else but lines that come to an end.

To give, then, image to the Imageless, for in depths
of the Real there is no ground, only fathomless sea,
life fashioned on the bedrock of the empty Abyss:

there, where the Source ceaselessly begets, un-begotten,
there, where the Love between breathes out and flows,
there, where the Mirror sees itself, Life-Giving-Life,

while light in its nakedness penetrates air, a plenitude,
like the dusk sky descended perfectly inside a cove,
the mind, now, observing, unguarded and un-walled.

(Imago)

But to discern God's will in this will o' the wisp world,
the seeming random daubs conjuring a picture whole,
ice melting, magnetism from dead metal, and time itself

a shatter of moments, phase shifted, from the everlasting
into these vectors of growth and decay: flatlanders aware,
unaware, endowed with a prized biological contraption

whereby they know *Nature does not act by purposes,*
that *Nature in itself has no reverence for life.*
And in your notebooks with the neat calculations,

graphs, your parsing of uncertainty, elliptical space,
those passages translated from Ruysbroeck's *Tabernacle:*
la lumière éternelle engloutissant toutes. . . une chaleur mystérieuse.

Shall we call it God's non-locality, every where at once,
that the eye altering the measure of light, this chamber eye,
misses, calibrated as it is for predator and prey.

Human being is an animal, you wrote, and human being
is a child of God: while in the animal world the transports
gain frequency, annihilated cargo, in this goldilocks world

with all the dials set for our arrival—luck like grace,
and Love like gravitation, a force, so the saint dreamed,
attracting the scattered sparks, jumbled puzzle, to Itself.

So in your house with friends you gather again to pray:
"Transcendence isn't passage; it's adding one life to another."
Light drawn to light in the image of every victim's face.

(Repertory)

The processional enters with its deliberate masques:
eight thousand generations, more or less, of diligent pain.
Though tonight in the theater it is Moliere, *Le Misanthrope,*

where the baseness of the species finds self-reproach.
You sit in the dark before the bright-lit proscenium
while outside, all around you, it is *Faust* playing out

without its second part to redeem the striving soul:
the flag, demonic, rippling in the public square, threats,
colleagues taken for forced labor, taken to the camps.

And you accused of being friends with Jews, the rector
seized for refusing to give the student names, the Jew,
Jesus, nailed again to the pattern of a crooked cross.

Enter Alceste: *That I could break with the human race.*
Do you follow back the drama to its first unfolding,
Australopithecus, Homo habilis, Home erectus, African Eve:

an original sin that's wired and woven, mitochondrial,
into the flesh, forgotten genocides, the dead ends,
along the long out-branching long ago of what we are?

Your mother in her seat shifts intently at your side.
Ascent? Descent? Encoded hate. Passivity. The guilt of it.
And the days ahead of discipline, prayer, the soul's work

of holding itself true—*forma omnium, materia omnium,*
essentia omnium, omnia sunt in ipsa divina essentia:
Everything that is, is in the very essence of God.

(Signature)

And the music of what happens? Hiss and battle strafe,
the flocks in rhythm over blood sluice and gas chamber.
In my father's house are many mansions. Thus in depths

of the rabbit hole you glimpse a flickering strobe:
Chance? Freedom? Divine life emptied into conditions,
dispossessed among the dispossessed, the dispossessing.

Thus: "God is hidden, hidden, even, from the beginning
of creation." Thus, too: what you called "the strangeness
of the universe," and relativity "a purely scientific matter

neither theistic nor atheistic, nothing whatsoever to do
with religion." To consider, then, the black body problem
where all light absorbed renders the object invisible:

or consciousness, as Schrödinger mused, liberated
from time by physical theory, and indestructible, our
senses unaccountable by the mind that requires them:

It resides upon them, is pieced together from them,
yet the mind cannot really be said to contain them.
While in the vacuum's zero all possible wavelengths

exist until they dazzle into tune and what is played
is played—a symphony, an open roll of the dice:
as now the bombers veer overhead, and your house

explodes around you, you alive in the mangled room.
Miracle? Ananke's chosen? Probability's favored child?
A God of the gulf, engulfing, not born of the gaps.

(Veil)

Robert Oppenheimer

"When they christened me secretly Rapid Rupture
I recalled the code my father taught me, *Deed before Creed*,
my aim to ensure the weapon as soon as prudent

but separating the isotope proved most impractical.
So we shifted from gun-type to a concerted design
that allowed the device to detonate by implosion.

We called it 'the Christy gadget,' after my student
who mapped the initiator for the chain reaction.
When Groves approved the test, our congregation

made its way to Ground Zero, not far from Pope:
White Sands, the range a kind of theater in the round,
lushly barren, sky blue as in a painting by Magritte.

At first I thought to place the weapon in its vessel,
spherical chalice, for containment, then opted to raise
the steel cup above to test the power. You know

what followed, though I'll quote again the Gita's lines:
*If the radiance of a thousand suns were to burst at once
into the sky, it would be like the splendor of the Mighty One.*

And after: desert burned to a green glass, Vishnu
transfigured in a version of Tabor—*I have become Death,
shatterer of worlds*, the clouds parting over Nagasaki.

I named the site Trinity to honor my old lover,
a suicide, its name from one of Donne's *Holy Sonnets*:
how the great artist separates light from darkness. . . ."

(Fractal)

And after the end the pat outbreak of rapture, the gone
taken into accountable absence, unaccountably vast:
the light years in atoms, the hair's breadth between stars.

Or picture a force newly rippling the vacuum, a field
risen like a violin's tuned strings, its harmonics and tones,
while outside the metal world every wave still exists

undetectable: metaphor for the dead, or for the living?
In city squares the crowds are rejoicing, the air infused
with summer's consequent light. You photograph them

as you photographed your room's obliterated walls,
will photograph your travels to Cape Town, Assisi,
in the world you'll know after a world's destroyed—

light through a shutter, paper, emulsion, the imprint
of time. To picture God's eye that singular camera,
or to picture four dimensions an infinite Now, ever-

lasting, forever complete and forever in passage,
a hologram splintered, fractal, the whole in each part.
In my father's house, He said, *are many mansions.*

Mansions in a house, as though the part happened
to out-build the whole? Let it be Brussels, 1945,
your innocuous apartment on the Rue de Braekeleer.

You sit in the sitting room reading your Ruysbroeck.
then turn to your piano, the one beloved and saved,
dusk through blinds, your fingers ranging the scales.

Of Motion, the Ever-Brightening Origin

What is man in nature? A nothing compared to the infinite, a whole
compared to the nothing, a middle point between all and nothing,
infinitely remote from any understanding of the extremes;
the end of things and their principles are unattainably hidden from him
in impenetrable secrecy. . . . What can he do, then, but perceive some
semblance of the middle of things, eternally hopeless of knowing either
their principles or their end? All things come out of nothing and are
carried onwards to infinity.

—Pascal

(Stream)

Jubilant billowing from the choir loft, throngs in song,
the faithful processing through the chapel's threshold,
bearing with them the statue, image of the apparition:

the sun dancing in its window in the clouds, the sun
a burning halo raining petals, in the center of its seal
Joseph with infant Jesus, around them daylight stars.

"How can one avoid being skeptical, Coimbra seeing
nothing of the witness, of the events at Fatima?"
You, caught in the crosshairs of your paths to truth:

piety and feasts, statistical notions, Masses and mass,
and energy immanent *in Galilean local coordinates*
while the universe speeds its breakneck transcendence,

the galaxies sanctuaries in recession without end.
So you saw lambda on the right hand not the left,
Einstein's crystalline sphere in pin-point balance

tipped from the equation: "The cosmological constant
may be compared to iron rods hidden inside a building,
indispensible to the structure of a synthesis more vast."

Saw photons decoupled into light in an instant's surge.
Saw horizons cooling and calibrated out of the fog.
Saw, before Oppenheimer, stars in radial collapse,

him leaving you un-cited. And the Princeton letter
with the master's judgment: *I am unable to believe
that such an ugly thing should be realized in nature.*

(Nexus)

To you even so comes the open door: to commune
with Einstein, Gödel, Bohr: and so to enter life
inside the magic circle, its vivid talk, your star again

in ascent, though the good son sadly begs to decline,
that future eclipsed behind the orbit of your duty.
Turn, then, to Pascal's double infinity, infinite depth,

infinite immensity, and nature a Janus face of cold
extremes, vast extents, where mind drifts uncertainly,
and everything seen *an imperceptible dot* stretched

above *the greater nothingness beyond our reach*—
seeing in him your shadow double, mathematician,
priest, drawn by both to the *astonishing processes.*

Observe: to derive a solution to the problem of three
bodies, in space or scalar field, how the perturbation
of one in motion with the other is caused by the third.

Observe: geometry at the quantum level is nonlocal,
the Planck threshold a phase from which spacetime
emerges, before which no space no time, nowhere.

Observe: Contrary to Pascal, one cannot deduce God
from infinite nature. Better to prefer *deus absconditus,*
God supremely inaccessible, hidden, unknowable.

But from the Unknowable, the known and its motion,
all in concert. *These extremes touch and join by going
in opposite directions, and meet in God, in God alone.*

(Contratemps)

All one, one would believe, and *Behind Every Door,*
God: the Pope in his prayerful speech bearing witness
to the august instant of the primordial Fiat Lux,

confirmation of the contingent universe from the hands
of the creator, well founded deduction, a bursting forth
from nothing into a sea of light, gesture of generous love.

Never, it appears, will you live it down, Pius's piety
the confirming gaffe, your "two paths" confused,
and you returned from Rome, bruising into class,

unlike (students noted) your irrepressibly cheerful self—
by your lights the primordial atom still unproven,
curtailed, perhaps, by an earlier stage of contraction

unaccounted for as yet in all empirical data, in all
the exacting equations clarifying a lens on the known:
the phoenix universe you entertained, "very beautiful."

Or the fact when wave functions collapse, it's the eye
parsing the probable into the real, extemporizing all
possible outcomes, many worlds, the real it turns out

more prodigal than Pascal's infinities, finitudes rolling
just beyond the glass edges of science and faith
in the bottoming abyss below before, now, and after

in which, in your time, you labor behind the scenes
to salvage the truth, its necessity, its separateness:
the fraught word of telling your infallible Pope no.

(Agnus)

George Gammow

"Mary had little lambda. His fleece was Jesus—Ha!
Of course, back in Odessa as child, I had to discover
for myself, so I take communion in Orthodox Church,

run home with bread and wine secreted in my cheek,
place it under microscope—I see no transubstantiation.
That's experiment that made me, Gamow, scientist.

Can you imagine, from hocus pocus to nucleosynthesis,
how in first five minutes light, dense particle soup,
recombines to form self, then bridges unbridgeable path

to make hydrogen, helium, all our heavier elements
without which no inflation, so no so called Big Bang
since priest could not account for equal values: stretch

of cosmic rays across scope of universe from this mix
I call *ylem*, from Middle English word for substance.
When Pope says this or Pope says that I have great fun,

add chunks of speech to my papers, watch eyebrows
rise, not God. But priest is excellent, better with math
than me, I admit, though he still believes in fairy tales.

It took atheist to see what must remain at radio end
of spectrum, and how his swelling lambda came to be,
I who with my wife once braved Black Sea in kayak

to escape Soviet Union—failure. How I'll never forget
sight of this dolphin I glimpsed through passing wave
illuminated, just then, by sun sinking below horizon."

(Anthropic)

This process of coming to life: autocatalysis of wave
to particle, particle to wave, from indeterminacy,
such that the photons fuse, the sun shines, the clay,

crystalline in its shallow pool, flickers into motion
so that in time the observer might observe, so that
in mind's conjuring what had come to be must be

brought before the mind as though it had not been,
could not be, until fashioned from the probabilities:
and all that might have been, too, fanning out deeply.

The theory says a lot, but does not really bring us any closer
to the secret of des Alten, the Old One, so Einstein
confided to Born. And now the master's dead is he

gifted with the Old One's secret, and your mother,
the windows of both their faces shaded and shut?
All goes onward and outward, nothing collapses—Whitman:

except the wave function out of its eternal now
below the proton's spin, before Planck's length waxes
from nothing, and nothing there until it's measured—

who measures the dead? *For our perpetual vows*
Canon Lemaître designed a brilliant course, how the life
of the mind carries the image of a nebula expanding,

spirit formed in contact with matter, the world-lines
of our becoming a further transcendence promising
what follows. Pure miracle? No. A phase. A threshold.

32

(Cinema)

In the film that doesn't begin and never ends, a man
wakes, drives to a country farmhouse where he finds
the guests he knows from his recurring dream, each

telling their own strange tale to him, the architect
called in to pitch his new design—a fratricidal son,
that ventriloquist whose dummy mouths his life–

progressive horror, till from his nightmare the man
wakes, drives to a country farmhouse where he finds
the guests he knows from his recurring dream. . . .

So with *Dead of Night*, Bondi, Gold, and Hoyle wake
to their design, the universe a Steady State, a cloud
that never moves from its mountaintop, one droplet

added for every one lost. Or like our own bodies
freshened cell by cell, creation continuous, God-less,
and atoms bred from atoms from alchemical stars.

You drive with Hoyle in the hills above Montalcino,
the cloth merchant's son, outspoken, caustic, truant,
who would label you comically "The Big Bang Man,"

arguing the probabilities: "What matter, Fred, creates
itself?" "Nothing, my dear Georges, then in an instant
a universe?" All that is, is, is spinning on a pencil point.

And you in his dinner portrait of you, a Friday fast,
coveting his steak, the enormous, undesired fish
appearing to stay the same size however much you eat.

(Spiritus)

Stylus, number wheel, gear tooth, cog, a falling weight
accomplishes the carry: So the years add up, interlocked,
as on a Pascaline to you at your Burroughs, desk-sized,

its circuits and sequences programmed with your code:
celestial mechanics as your students crowd the bulk,
nebulae cast in binaries coalescing from the expanse,

and the calibrated universe shaped as by an algorithm,
the way crystal calculates to crystal, self-generating,
ramified in solution, salt, pattern, Adamic brick and clay.

Let it be, then, Ruysbroeck's *sparkling stone*, emergent
in matter's ontogeny, a seeded cascade into sentience,
the code in us that shows, you believed, "the universe

is not out of reach. . . this is Eden, garden that grows
so that it might see." Let it be Newton's miracle pin
balanced on its mirror, the possible impossibility: be

the emptying, first flash like foxfire quickened out
of Nil, catalytic light unfurling into net—galaxies,
planets—where the iterative urge burgeons into soul,

pebble on which its new name will be written, the holy
contracted into panoply, an extrication, the risk
of immanence: dewdrop pendant on a grass blade, the

suffering one forsaken on his deliberate tree. And you
in your *jouissance* parsing assemblers, your *Hoc est Corpus*
at the Mass, the *riffraff* in the *ylem* winnowing up.

(Corpus)

For all of it, how presumptuous, we thinking reeds,
unable as we are to stand outside the human, the cost
of our becoming, all becoming, a ripple of sun across

the leopard's back as it locks on the gazelle, prodigal
orders of blood and contingency, signifying nothing.
Or, if not, a hidden sum in the corpus of the random.

Each evening, after class, out with the student throng,
you carry, boisterous, your conversations to the cafes,
take your meals at the Majestic, comfortable routine.

And when the violence comes, like a recessive flaw
in the source code of history, the binaries—Flemish,
Walloon—shatter again your safe sphere with bricks

through your windows for having counseled peace.
Cape Town, Chicago, Berkeley, Milan, Rome—unreal
the life passing, and you ready with your camera

limning the moment, taking its measure, gradations
of light and shade, companions, vistas, incalculable
the event horizon of the present arrowing on ahead

and tied to a promise, Augustine knew, by memory:
that time, Paris, your trip to program the new machine,
hours at it, and afterwards till almost dawn your beers

with friends, you in your soutane walking wryly past
the flagrant women, the Moulin Rouge, your big laugh
explosive in the lobby: "We have been to the Pigalle!"

(Canto)

Is it motion itself that makes the day? Or is it the time
taken by that motion? Or is it both? the saint asked,
searchingly—*Deus creator omnium*: the measure

of mind made by the Maker of minds, and time
come to existence only observable as time, phase
transition to the radio spectrum, pre–recombinant,

the primordial light unchanged from the initial
sea of light, a television hiss homing everywhere,
mysterious, incessant: as to this twenty-foot horn

where the pigeons have posited their nest, where
their white dielectric material seems the source.
And Penzias, son of Polish Jews, born the day

the Gestapo formed, his father a janitor stoking
furnaces in the Bronx, scrubs the antenna clean,
again adjusts the cold load grounding the array.

And knows what he hears is light's first word
through time's wall, un-walled. And you, the priest
who foreknew it, envisioned this omnipresence

equation after equation, recline a little easier
into your death bed at the news, the diminuendo
never ending, the under-melody of a symphony

distantly keyed, like the tune the saint heard, *prior*
to origin, since a song is not given form to become sound,
but sound given form to become song: You enter the song.

(Matins)
Georges Lemaître

"*Mon ami, mon frère,* in the trenches nearly *mon semblable,*
Georges et Georges, though you changed back to *Joris*
to claim outright your Flemish past, a Flemish future,

let this be my last letter to you if only in my mind.
Into every horizon brims the ancient light one hears
like a primal score, before which everything evolves.

To think then of the infinite lives, each entangled,
like yours and mine, never to be separated despite,
Van Severen, the severances passing: us at the front

with our Bibles, our Bloy, his passion for the poor,
for justice, you with your felt wrongs, your drive
for redress by which you fashioned your visionary

gleam, self cult, the Fascist idol for which you died.
I preferred my silent retreats, my Poincaré, the dual
certitude of a double path, divergent, to the Truth.

Still, I pray I might have turned you from that road,
a tragic strut, your bit part on time's proscenium.
I have had my journey, too, and have followed it

faithfully, a rightness, like the eclipse I witnessed
before my own came on: the observatory in Milan,
that halo when the three bodies perfectly aligned,

not only in equations but in flesh. We are all strayed
lines in an infinite story we see, at best, darkly.
The rooster crows and thinks it makes the sun rise."

(Cove)

Sometimes it's no different than the sound of the surf,
this key of light breaking on the shore of everything,
whisper conjured out of vacuum and hush, fathomless.

On the night you died the waves were lifting, the sands
a shifting membrane at Gravelines, Calais, the North Sea
one sea, and the sands multiplying myriad after myriad

falling short of infinity. So make each grain a universe,
each universe an origin that billows into next and next,
while each in its time, in its merciless time, waxes old

like a garment, and hastens out of sight. Now, this now,
a white heron stands at water's edge beside the inlet,
and those gathered on the walk, on the beach, pass by

un-regarding, private orbits of need and happenstance
coming to be, gathering in patterns, windfalls of seeds
along the jigsaw of a jetty—rockroses in the cracks,

delicate blooms. And of that other Now, measureless,
below the threshold of every knowing? "The evolution
of Providence," you said, "does not exclude the physical,

this living world with its random mutations, its accidence
harboring toward a goal." Is it risen, or descended,
this manifold mirror of bay and sky, horizon-less,

utterly still, utterly in motion, held, stretching across,
offered like a cup? A lifting, unencumbered, of wings.
At dawn a blood-red host; a blood-red host at nightfall.

. . .and the universe nothing more than dream;
and we, blind as book lice, cross the slight

horizon of a page, to miss the moment
in our desperate flittering, the Word unread,

sustaining, beneath us: purpose and path—
ash to amethyst, moth wing, seraph, breath. . .

NOTES

Titles and Quotations
The Most Ancient Light in the Most Ancient Sky (Sections I- XI)—is from
Wallace Stevens' "Ordinary Evening in New Haven." *The Death of One God
is the Death of All* (XII-XXII) is from Stevens' "Notes Toward a Supreme
Fiction;" and *Of Motion the Ever-Brightening Origin* (XXIII- XXXIII) is from
Stevens' "The Auroras of Autumn." The quotation preceding *The Most Ancient
Light in the Most Ancient Sky* is from Georges Lemaître "The Primeval Atom;"
the quotations preceding *The Death of One God is the Death of All* are from
Albert Einstein's *Life and Opinions*; the quotation preceding *Of Motion the
Ever-Brightening Origin* is from Pascal's *Pensees*.

SECTIONS
(Fountain)
Perihelion: point of orbit of a planet when it is nearest the sun; *Cepheid*:
variable or pulsating star whose luminosity helps chart distances in space. The
lines in italics are paraphrased from Lemaître's early essay on the primeval
atom.
(Origin)
Lemaître's father, Joseph, owned a factory in Charleroi, 173 miles south
of Brussels. He invented a new procedure for "stretching" glass. When the
factory was destroyed he borrowed from family to pay back his employees and
creditors after which he moved the family to Brussels and practiced law.
(Fiat)
Lemaître fought in the Battle of the Yser, one of the most horrific of the First
World War. For meritorious service he received the Croix de Guerre.
(De Rerum)
Jules Henri Poincaré (1854-1912): French mathematician, physicist, and engineer
who among many innovations introduced the modern concept of relativity.
(Parallax)
Introibo ad altare Dei. Ad Gloriam: In the Latin Mass, "I will go to the altar of
God," "To the glory of." *Karl Schwartzchild* (1873-1916), German physicist,
provided the Schwartzchild solution for rotating masses anticipating black
hole theory; *Henry Moseley* (1887-1915), English physicist, famous for
Moseley's law on the X-ray spectra that helps organize the chemistry of the
periodic table according to physical law; *Willem De Sitter* (1872-1934), Dutch
mathematician whose so called De Sitter Universe provides a cosmological
model for Einstein's general relativity requiring a universe without matter.

(Trajectory)
Puranas: ancient Sanskrit religious text sacred to Hindus and Buddhists;
Arthur Eddington (1882-1944), English physicist and earlier champion
of relativity theory and Lemaître's theory of the "primeval atom;" *Sobral,
Principe*: destinations for the 1919 expeditions for the solar eclipse which
proved Einstein's prediction of relativity theory correct; *Bottom:* character in
Shakespeare's *A Midsummer's Night's Dream*
(Scope)
Harlow Shapely (1885-1972), American astronomer, who initially believed
nebulae were part of the Milky Way and not galaxies in their own right; *Vesto
Slipher* (1875-1969), American astronomer.
(Vector)
Erwin Schrödinger (1887-1961), German physicist and biologist and one of
the founders of quantum mechanics, famous for Schrödinger's equation
establishing the "wave function" of matter illustrated by the famous thought
experiment known popularly as "Schrödinger's Cat."
(Proscenium)
Albert Einstein (1879-1955); *Solvay:* Conference on Physics and Chemistry
held in Brussels, 1927.
(Observance)
Edwin Hubble (1889-1953), American astronomer who discovered that the
degree of Doppler shift (red shift) is directly proportional to the speed at
which galaxies are speeding away from the earth, thereby establishing the
fact that the universe is expanding; *Milton Humason* (1891-1974), American
astronomer.
(Shore)
The excerpts are from Einstein's *Ideas and Opinions* (New York: Crown, 1982).
(Melisma)
Hitler's mountain residence was in Berchtesgaden. On November 19, 1940
King Leopold of Belgium officially capitulated to the German Reich.
(Calculus)
Kurt Asche (1909-1998) oversaw the deportation of Belgian Jews to Auschwitz
at the Micheline internment camp north of Brussels; *Jozef-Ernest Van Roey*
(1874-1961): Belgian Cardinal who publically opposed Nazi Germany and
encouraged resistance against the occupying forces.
(Chamber)
Pope Pius XII, Eugenio Pacelli (1876-1958): controversial figure whose
decisions during the Second World War to avoid direct confrontation with
Hitler have caused him to be condemned in some quarters, while other

scholars have praised his work to save Jews covertly without inciting further violence or endangering the Catholic Church; Jews were required to wear yellow stars in Nazi occupied Europe. Details from this section are derived from Jose Sanchez's even-handed book *Pius XII and the Holocaust*.
(Aperture)
The first thought experiment is posed by Frank Close in his book *The Void*; *Gregor Mendel* (1822-1884): Augustinian Monk, founder of the science of genetics.
(Tenebrae)
The first stanza riffs a phrase from Brian Greene's *The Elegant Universe*; *Der Alte*: "The Old One," Einstein's preferred appellation for God; *Newton's Divine Observer*: Sir Isaac Newton speculated that space might be filled with a spiritual substance and called space "the divine observatory."
(Sanctum)
Jan van Ruysbroeck 14th Century mystic and author of *The Spiritual Espousals* and *The Sparkling Stone* (among other works) from which these paraphrases are taken.
(Imago)
Heisenberg's uncertainty principle maintains that in binaries of physical properties, the more one property is measured the less the other property can be determined—light behaving as either wave or particle but not both simultaneously; the lines in italics are taken from Edwin Schrödinger's *What is Life?* The translation from the French is: "Eternal light engulfing all. . . a mysterious heat." In his notebooks Lemaître copied and offered commentary on extensive passages from Ruysbroeck's writings.
(Repertory)
The species homo sapiens emerges about 160,000 years ago, so about 5000 generations; Lemaître was a devotee of Moliere's plays, but believed the plays to have been written in fact by Louis XIV; *forma omnium, materia omnium, / essentia omnium, omnia sunt in ipsa divina essential*:: "the form of things," "the matter of things," "the essence of things" "all things exist in the very essence of God"—these are each theological formulas articulating God's relation to creation, as discussed in Josef Zycinski's *God and Evolution*; the quotation at the bottom of the page is from Ruysbroeck's *The Spiritual Espousals*.
(Signature)
Apart from the biblical quotation in the first stanza the remaining italicized phrases are taken from Lemaître's archives at the university of Louvain-la-Neuve. The quoted lines are from Schrödinger's *What is Life*. Lemaître's house was bombed inadvertently by U.S. warplanes in 1944; he narrowly escaped with his life; *Ananke*: Greek for "necessity."

(Veil)

J. Robert Oppenheimer (1904-1967) presided over the development of the atomic bomb during the Second World War, known as the Manhattan Project. Rapid Rupture was his code name; *Lieutenant General R. Leslie Groves* (1896-1970), military director of the Manhattan Project; *Jean Tatlock* was Oppenheimer's lover before and after his marriage; she committed suicide in 1944 after introducing Oppenheimer to Donne's Holy Sonnets; *Robert Christy* (1916-2012), American astrophysicist; *Tabor:* mountain in Israel and site of the biblical transfiguration of Jesus.

(Fractal)

Rue de Braekeleer is in Brussels, Belgium.

(Stream)

Fatima: The Feast of Our Lady of Fatima, May 13, commemorating the apparitions of the Virgin Mary in Portugal in 1917; *Coimbra:* observatory in Portugal; *Galilean coordinates:* after Galileo, coordinates used to transform between two reference frames in space. The word Galilean also has another intended incidental reference.

(Nexus)

After the Second World War Lemaître was asked to join the Institute for Advanced Studies at Princeton to join Einstein and other notable scientists; he declined out of deference to taking care of his elderly mother. Kurt Gödel (1906-1978), Austrian mathematician and philosopher, and Niels Bohr (1885-1962), Danish physicist and one of the founders of quantum mechanics, spent time with Einstein at the Institute for Advanced Studies in Princeton; the first observation sketches the "three body problem in physics; *Planck threshold:* the Planck length is the tiniest unit of physical reality, named after Max Plank (1858-1947), German physicist; Blaise Pascal (1623-1662), French mathematician and philosopher. The quotation in the last stanza of this section is from his *Pensées.*

(Contratemps)

The opening stanza paraphrases Pius XII's speech to the Pontifical Academy of Sciences.

(Agnus)

George Gamow (1904-1968), Russian physicist who championed the idea of an expanding universe and discovered, among other things, the process by which hydrogen atoms decay, thereby presaging the inflation theory of universal expansion developed by Alan Guth. It is said he never used articles when he spoke in English.

(Anthropic)
Max Born (1882-1970), German physicist and developer of quantum mechanics. The lines in quotation paraphrase the recollection of one of Lemaître's students at the retreat.

(Cinema)
Hermann Bondi (1919-2005), German-born physicist and mathematician; Thomas Gold (1920-2004) Austrian-born physicist; and Fred Hoyle (1915-2001), English physicist, developed the Steady State theory of the universe after watching the English film *Dead of Night* in 1946. Hoyle and Lemaître traveled in Italy together in 1957, recounted in Hoyle's memoir, *Home is Where the Wind Blows*.

(Spiritus)
Pascaline: the name of given by Blaise Pascal to the mechanical calculator he invented in 1642; Newton's "miracle pin": Sir Isaac Newton envisioned the precise calibration of the universe as a pin balancing precisely on the smooth surface of a mirror. I affiliate that precision with the concept of Logos, which also has religious implications; *sparkling stone*: title of Ruysbroeck's mystical treatise, from the biblical Book of Revelation 2: 17; *Hoc est corpus*: Latin for "This is my body," the words recited by the priest he raises the host in the Tridentine Mass; *riffraff*: Old English word for "particles"; *yelm*: Old English word for "substance" used by George Gamow for the early plasma of the universe.

(Corpus)
"Thinking reeds" is Pascal's phrase. In the early 1960s the University of Louvain faced a crisis when the Flemish students and faculty wanted to separate into a Dutch-speaking university, reflecting long-standing historical conflicts in Belgian society between French-speaking Walloons and the Flemish. Lemaître supported keeping the university together. The windows of his house were smashed with bricks in protest. The Catholic University of Leuven became entirely Dutch-speaking in 1968; Louvain-la-Neuve began construction in 1971.

(Canto)
The opening lines paraphrase Augustine's *Confessions*; *Deus creator omnium*: "God that created all things," a hymn for Saturday vespers; Arno Penzias (1933), American Physicist born in Poland, who with James Wilson (1936-2000) discovered the cosmic background microwave radiation in 1964 while working at Bell Labs in New Jersey. Penzias's father owned a leather business in Poland before escaping with his family. The italicized lines in the final stanza also paraphrase Augustine's *Confessions*.

(Matins)
Van Severen: Joris Van Severen (1894-1940), was a close friend of Lemaître's in the trenches of World War I and became a vocal member of the Front Movement of Flemish soldiers who were ardent Flemish nationalists. They shared a Catholic faith inspired by Leon Bloy (1846-1917), the French religious philosopher and advocate for the poor. Severen and Lemaître's friendship dissolved as Van Severen became more radical in his politics, eventually gravitating to right wing sympathies. He was executed in 1940 by French soldiers.
(Cove)
The first line riffs Arnold Penzias's recollection of hearing the CMB, the cosmic microwave background radiation; the italicized lines are paraphrased from the final interview given by Lemaître two weeks before his death.

ACKNOWLEDGEMENTS

*Alabama Literary Review, Ibbetson Street, Irish Pages, JMWW,
Notre Dame Review, Pennine Platform, Plume, Spiritus,* and
Tiferet.

Three works were essential to the making of this poem: John Farrell's *The
Day Without Yesterday: Lemaître, Einstein, and the Birth of Modern Cosmology*,
Dominque Lambert's *L'Itineraire Spirituel de Georges Lemaître*, and Valerie
De Rath's *George Lemaître, le Pere du Big Bang*, as well as Lemaître's own
writings and notebooks. *From Nothing* would not have been written
without the enormous generosity and personal attention of Liliane
Moens-Haulotte, Director of the Archives Georges Lemaître at the
University of Louvain-La-Neuve, Belgium, her husband Michel Haulotte,
Gilbert Lemaître who provided important insight into his uncle's life,
and Christine Casson who was instrumental in assisting with the research
as well as offering inspiration and an impeccable ear. *From Nothing* is
dedicated to them.

I am also grateful for the helpful readership of Bruce Beasley, Mari Coates,
Hamida Bosmajian, Martha Rhodes, William B. Thompson and William
Wenthe. I would also like to thank Harlan Bosmajian for the making of
his short film based on this poem.

Daniel Tobin is the author of seven books of poems, *Where the World is Made, Double Life, The Narrows, Second Things, Belated Heavens* (winner of the Massachusetts Book Award in Poetry), *The Net*, and *From Nothing*. He is also the author of the critical studies *Passage to the Center: Imagination and the Sacred in the Poetry of Seamus Heaney* and *Awake in America*, as well as the editor of *The Book of Irish American Poetry from the Eighteenth Century to the Present, Light in Hand: The Selected Early Poems and Lola Ridge*, and *Poet's Work, Poet's Play: Essays on the Practice and the Art*. His awards include the "The Discovery/The Nation Award," the Robert Penn Warren Award, the Robert Frost Fellowship, the Katherine Bakeless Nason Prize, and fellowships in poetry from the National Endowment for the Arts and the John Simon Guggenheim Foundation. This book would not have been written without the generous support of a fellowship in poetry from the John Simon Guggenheim Foundation and Four Way Books which provided a month-long residency at the Fine Arts Work Center in Provincetown.

Publication of this book was made possible by grants and donations. We are also grateful to those individuals who participated in our 2015 Build a Book Program. They are:

Jan Bender-Zanoni, Betsy Bonner, Deirdre Brill, Carla & Stephen Carlson, Liza Charlesworth, Catherine Degraw & Michael Connor, Greg Egan, Martha Webster & Robert Fuentes, Anthony Guetti, Hermann Hesse, Deming Holleran, Joy Jones, Katie Childs & Josh Kalscheur, Michelle King, David Lee, Howard Levy, Jillian Lewis, Juliana Lewis, Owen Lewis, Alice St. Claire Long & David Long, Catherine McArthur, Nathan McClain, Carolyn Murdoch, Tracey Orick, Kathleen Ossip, Eileen Pollack, Barbara Preminger, Vinode Ramgopal, Roni Schotter, Soraya Shalforoosh, Marjorie & Lew Tesser, David Tze, Abby Wender, and Leah Nanako Winkler